OneEssence
The Nondual Clarity of an Ancient Zen Poem.

Robert Wolfe on the Hsin Hsin Ming.

Karina Library Press, 2011
Ojai, California

One Essence: The Nondual Clarity of an Ancient Zen Poem.
print edition, ISBN-13: 978-0-9824491-7-2
ebook edition, ISBN-13: 978-0-9824491-8-9

Editor: Michael Lommel, michael@karinalibrary.com

Library of Congress Control Number: 2011933015

Karina Library Press
PO Box 35
Ojai, California 93024

www.karinalibrary.com

Book designed in ComputerModern Sans (Donald Knuth) and
OpenType Baskerville.

Also by Robert Wolfe

Living Nonduality:
Enlightenment Teachings of Self-Realization

The Gospel of Thomas:
The Enlightenment Teachings of Jesus

www.livingnonduality.org

Sign up for free updates on new titles:
www.karinalibrary.com/newsletter

Preface 1

Introduction 7

1. *The Way* 11

2. *Enlightened Advice* 15

3. *Conflict of Opposites* 19

4. *Formlessness* 25

5. *Empty Mind* 29

6. *Silent Mind* 35

7. *Dream World* 39

8. *Not two, nor one* 43

9. *No self, no mind* 47

10. *Namelessness* 53

11. *Come what may* 57

12. *Equanimity* 61

13. *Undivided* 65

14. *All-encompassing* 71

15. *Timeless* 75

16. *Essence* 79

Addenda 83

In Death as in Life 105

Dedicated to Jerry Jones.

The original face is limitless;
It cannot be probed by mind.

True enlightenment is not enlightenment,
Real emptiness is not empty.

Niu T'ou (7th c.)

Preface

The lyric expressions of enlightenment, over the eons, have had an influential effect on many persons, in many places—including myself. Some examples follow.

Robert Wolfe
Ojai, California

The presence that pervades the universe
is imperishable, unchanging—
beyond both *is* and *is not*: how could it ever vanish?
Bhagavad Gita

His mind is empty.
He is not concerned with meditation,
or the absence of it,
or the struggle between "good" and "evil".

Ashtavakra Gita

Seek the wisdom that will untie your knot;
seek the path that demands your whole being.
Leave that which is *not*, but appears to be;
seek that which *is*, but is not apparent.

Rumi

As long as I am this or that, or "have" this or that,
  I am not all things and I have not all things.
(When) you neither *are* nor have this or that,
  then you are omnipresent and—being *neither*
this nor that—are all things.

Meister Eckhart

In order to arrive
at being everything,
desire to be nothing.

John of the Cross

Introduction

Hui Neng, the Sixth Chinese Patriarch, is said to have been an illiterate woodcutter who was enlightened delivering wood, upon hearing his customer chanting a sutra verse. The enduring inspiration of spiritual verse, though such a profound occurrence may be rare, perhaps accounts for its perennial revival—like flowers among a scriptural forest.

The unrhymed, aphoristic couplets that comprise the Hsin Hsin Ming have a time-honored niche in the transmission of the dharma. (It is even the basis for some of the classic koan riddles.) If you know of a particular translated version, you might find it beneficial to read it alongside the one given in the following pages. There are more than a dozen English variants available, and I have utilized the phrasing of some of these alternates to deepen the nuance of a passage, when possible. A few of the extant renditions I have paraphrased for brevity. And a common word that is sometimes capitalized is meant to indicate that it is a descriptive word pointing to the ultimate Reality.

In this day, when the teachings of nonduality are being scrutinized by a growing public, the Hsin Hsin Ming again casts its reflective light on another generation privileged to contemplate its clarity and directness.

The Way

1.

The Tao is self-evident
To those who live in choiceless awareness.

When you perceive everything objectively,
Your path is clear and unobstructed.

THUS BEGIN THE VERSES OF THE HSIN HSIN MING. Or, at least, thus begins this version of the translation of it.* Like the Dao de jing (known in previous years as the Tao te Ching),† this classic spiritual scripture has undergone many translations over the centuries. Consequently, the interpretation of its original wording has varied in each rendition.‡ But the central, emphatic message remains consistently clear throughout its text: the importance and value of comprehending the nondual perspective.

The word *Tao* (or *Dao*) basically means Way, in the sense of a direction, or passage, or opening. We might say that to pass through the transcendental opening is to embrace the Tao, to find one's unencumbered way in this life on earth.

---

* This version was provided to me by a correspondent, who based its composition on existing versions he had studied.

† The *Dao de jing* is thought to have been composed circa 600 B.C., in China, reputedly by Lao tzu.

‡ An example of the flexibility in translating Chinese characters: *Cheng tao* can be rendered "experience of enlightenment" or "proving the Way."

In Buddhism, this path is said to lead us to encounter the "gateless gate," the point at which the disciple experiences no obstructions.*

Most often, in the translations of this Zen text,† the opening words are given as the Great Way, or Supreme or Perfect Way, in the sense of "ultimate," or transcendent or Absolute. An alternate usage for Way or Tao is Mind (or Buddha Mind), again a reference to the universal or absolute Presence which knows no limitation.

Hsin, in the poem's title, indicates (in one sense of its usage) Mind, as a formless Presence which is the source of all being. As used in a second sense, Hsin also refers to an awareness of this ubiquitous Presence, to the extent of realizing one's identity with it, thus generating a complete trust in the omnipresent Mind. In the trust of this Mind, there is no separation from it, no dissimilarity: Hsin Hsin.

Ming is a "treatise," a teaching; in this case, in a versified format similar to the Dao de jing or the Sermon on the Mount. So the title of the Hsin Hsin Ming has been translated variously as (for instance) Affirming the Buddha-Mind, or The Mind of Absolute Trust.

Let's look at the second stanza; consider the origin of the poem; and then explore these initial admonitions in greater depth.

---

* What Suzuki Roshi said of a similar Zen poem, written by the Eighth Chinese Patriarch, applies to the Hsin Hsin Ming: "When a Buddhist reads it, it is a Buddhist text, and when a Daoist reads it, it is a Daoist text."

† Zen is the Japanese name for what was originally called Ch'an in China. And Shin Jin Mei is the Japanese name for the Hsin Hsin Ming.

Enlightened Advice

2.

When you deviate from it,
You fall into duality.

If you want to comprehend the Tao,
Remain impartial.

BUDDHIST TRADITION ASCRIBES the authorship of the Hsin Hsin Ming to Chien-chih Seng Ts'an (also called, by the Japanese, Kanchi Sosan, or Sosan Zenji). He is considered to be the third successive Chinese "patriarch," * or dharma heir, and the 30th successor in a lineage tracing itself back to the Buddha (who illumined India in the period around 550 B.C.).

Not all Buddhist scholars agree with the attribution of this text to Seng Ts'an. Some feel it may have been written after 606 A.D., the year when the Third Patriarch died.

Part of the problem with attributing the Hsin Hsin Ming to Seng Ts'an is that so little is known about him. When we set aside the mythical tales which typically attach to venerable spiritual figures, all we can reliably say is that Seng Ts'an was considered, like Buddha, to have been enlightened. And so, we can say of the author of the Hsin Hsin Ming only that he (assuming it was not a she) is pointing to a needle's eye through which he himself evidently has passed. Regardless of its authorship, enlightenment teachers throughout the past centuries have cited the poem as a touchstone, right up to the present day. †

---

* The "First Patriarch" is said to be Bodhidharma, alleged to have brought the essence of Zen precepts to Taoist China circa 520 A.D.

† Two commentaries within the past 20 years, in English: *The Eye Never Sleeps,* by Dennis Genpo Merzel, a successor of Zen master Maezumi Roshi; and *Faith in Mind* by Chinese Zen master Sheng Yen. Both contain commentaries. The oft-cited translation of Richard B. Clarke (adopted by Merzel), himself a dharma teacher, is available as an 8-page booklet also. Clarke's appraisal of the poem: "The essence of Zen. This is all you need."

While the path is "clear and unobstructed," there is an essential reason why it may not seems so. For that reason, the poem's author wrote 146 (four-character) lines, comprising about 30 verses. The theme is repetitive throughout: impartial, choiceless perception. And the contrary perception is clear throughout: to "fall into duality."

Let us add the next two verses, then consider all the first four, from the beginning.

Conflict of Opposites

3.

Not accepting things as they are
Leads to mental imbalance.

When you fail to accord with the Tao,
Peace of mind is lost.

The Tao is limitless as space
With nothing missing, nothing superfluous.

If you do not accept things as they are,
You will fail to comprehend the nature of things.

THE FIRST FOUR LINES of the very first verse (Chapter 1) are warning us, at the start, to be wary of attachment to preferences; to be aware of our conditioned tendency to judge all things on a spectrum that ranges from positive to negative. This means to take notice of the things which we like and which we dislike, and of our impulse to either "accept" or "reject" what appears before us moment by moment. Such preferential choices are at the root of both love and hate; at the root of ambition as well as greed; at the root of the exclusiveness known as selfishness.

The issue here is not simply to live in "awareness" of what presents itself to you daily, but in objective, nonjudgmental awareness. In such perceptive awareness, conflict ceases to arise; your path is unobstructed, clear.

The next four lines that follow the beginning verse (Chapter 2) warn us of the consequence when we deviate from awareness that has been emptied of choice: the Way is obstructed by duality.

From your days as an infant, you have been conditioned to distinguish everything you encounter by identifying each object with a separate name. Each of these names limits an object to a particular conceived form, creating a self-imposed boundary—boundaries in a reality which, in the absence of such divisive, definitional names, is simply One.

This is best said by one of the alternate translations:

> Cling to a hairbreadth of distinction
> and 'heaven' and 'earth' are set apart.

In other words, the inseparable and seamless One is now broken into "God" and "man." And the Being which is common to us all is now divided as "you" and "I."

When we are bound up in the dualistic perspective, the distinctions we make between "good" and "bad," "right" and "wrong" and "better" or "worse" can lead only to oppositional and conflicting choices. This is to fail to "comprehend" the transcendental Way. As a translation puts it:

> To perceive Reality as it is,
> live with an open mind.

Put another way, Truth is not a matter of opinion; Reality is not dependent on whether we're "for" or "against" it. So only when you end your contentious mindset can peace of mind prevail, and both internal and external turmoil subside. Or, as one of the translations says:

> Not to see the Way's deep truth
> disturbs the mind's essential peace.

And this also applies to social peace, as indicated by an additional translation:

> Misunderstanding the great Mystery,
> people labor in vain for peace.

Through accord with the One, you remove self-limitation and self-centeredness, and you open to the unfolding of a Totality which can't be revealed by grasping for it. In the words of a translation:

> Fix your mind on part of it
> and you will miss the whole of it.

What can we say of this Totality—and of our being in accord with it? And how do the poem's phrases "void" and "emptiness" relate to this One?

Formlessness

4.

Detach from both worldly things
And the inner void.

Be serene in their oneness,
And dualism vanishes by itself.

S PIRITUAL AND RELIGIOUS TRADITIONS throughout the ages have directed our attention to the One, to an Absolute presence or be-ing. In different times and places, this has received varying names: God, Brahman, Tao, Mind, Self, and so forth. Various adjectives have been appended to these names: infinite, eternal, omnipresent, formless, empty.

All material (and even immaterial) forms—"the ten thousand things," as Buddhists generalize it—seemingly arise from a "ground of being" which itself is beyond any such limitation as form. By its nature, enlightened seers have consistently averred, the Formless—being infinite or limitless in every reach of space or time—is without boundaries or restraints. Therefore, this omnipresent Reality not only surrounds every perceptible object, but penetrates and saturates everything, as well. It is this ubiquitous Presence which connects all things in an underlying commonality, and gives "oneness," universality, its meaning.

This formless Presence is not, itself, a limited entity or "thing." It cannot be identified except as the essence of all which manifests from (or rather, as) this source: all that we view as temporal objects, including each person, is essentially and inherently It.

Having no separable identity of its own, it is said to be "void," or "empty" of discernible features. Yet is it this void, or formless condition, from which all else appears and into which every thing ultimately disappears.

Some seers refer to the impermanent, material appearances as "unreal"—as are those observed figures in our sleeping dreams—and consider the "empty" void to be, due to its permanent presence, the only Reality.

Every entity, every form (even conceptual forms), is limited to, and by, its description: each derives its identity or definition in relation to all the other things in the universe which it is not. In other words, as has been said, "every thing is relative."

The all-inclusive Formless is said to be non-relative, being independent of all other factors for its origination. A word whose precise definition is "not relative," Absolute is the term which has been applied in spiritual traditions generally, over the ages.

The designations "relative" and "Absolute" are often seen together, which falsely may give the impression that each is a description of a separate condition, or to be differentiated from one another. But various scriptures mean to remind us that all that is relative exists within the condition of the Absolute—simultaneously as the Absolute exists within all that is relative. The "two" are inseparable, merely aspects of the ubiquitous One.

Thus you see expressions such as, "form [the relative] is emptiness [the Absolute or Void], emptiness is form"; or even, "All is One, One is All." In other words, in regard to the Totality there are no "parts"; the parts are merely its myriad appearances as formations of this indivisible whole.

Hence, the teachings of nonduality remind us that while our (conditioned) dualistic perception has practical value in a material world of discernible objects, "Fix your mind on part of It, and you will miss the whole of It." See a dichotomy, and a choice to be made, between the "holy" and the "profane," and you are caught up in a dualistic conflict. Transcend such separative categories, and you "live in choiceless awareness... accept things as they are...comprehend the nature of things" and "accord with the Tao." In perceiving Oneness, more importantly, "dualism vanishes by itself," without your concern and effort.

Empty Mind

5.

Trying to maintain stillness
Leads to agitation.

If you do not accept things as they are,
How can you realize oneness?

And when oneness is not realized,
You fall into error.

Reject reality, and you lose touch with it.
Plunge into the void, and you find only emptiness.

IN SOME SPIRITUAL DISCIPLINES, an effort is made to control or restrict the normal workings of the mind. As this poem's author reiterates, where nonduality is not thoroughly comprehended, a person will seek to apprehend ultimate Reality outside oneself as some remote state eventually to be encountered. We already, nondual scripture tells us—by its presence in and around all that is—accord with ultimate Reality. It is imminently inescapable. Whether we are aware of it or not. As the Vedic scriptures profess, Tat tvam asi: "That [omnipresent Reality] thou art." Not "will someday be," but are now.

The principle argument advanced for concentrating one's attention on the vagaries of the meandering mind is that, by so doing, one will eventually become aware of ultimate Reality as an innate condition in a quiescent psyche. However, where it is recognized that this Reality is the source and expression of every conceivable object or form—as well as any effect, purpose or activities of these phenomenon—it is clear that no effort or discipline will make manifest that which already is incumbent as the fundamental essence of all that is (whether material or immaterial).

To judge the normal tendencies of mental activity to be somehow inimical or inappropriate, or out of accord with Reality, and to choose as an objective a state or condition in preference to what presently exists, is to be caught up in incipient duality.

Four alternate translations, of the preceding couplets, instruct us:

Trying to still the mind
inhibits the experience of Oneness.

Try to stop activity to achieve quietude,
and your very effort will fill you with activity.

Reside in the Oneness of things,
where distinctions are meaningless.

In the equanimity of absolute Oneness,
confusion vanishes by itself.

There is, as a consequence of nondual awareness, a "stillness" which is not in opposition to "agitation," but instead an open expanse in which any and all conditions are freely permitted to appear.

Where there is explicit trust in the harmonious processes of Reality, one's all-encompassing awareness will recognize that "creation" and "destruction," "desirable" and "undesirable," "stillness" and "turmoil"—and any other seeming bifurcations—are all merely varying elements in the unfolding of the One.

As a consequence of the transcendence of concern about the nature of whatever condition is present, one recognizes that ultimately none of the impermanent phenomena matter: "all things change"; the truly still mind merely attunes to Reality in all its diverse forms and appearances, and views "things as they are" with neutrality and an instinctual non-interference. The stillness in this mind requires no effort to maintain; no time to inculcate, no practitioner to be perfected.

Following are two alternate translations of verses we've considered so far:

If you do not recognize the one Mind,
opposites will lead you nowhere.

If you hold onto opposites,
how can you understand One?

The mind that is thus still, by its nature, is said to be an
"empty" mind—free of opinions, abstract conceptualizations,
ideas about how things "should" be. It does not dwell in the
past with what "has been," rather than "what is"; it tends
not to project a future, thus exciting neither apprehension
nor anticipation. Aside from practical matters, mentation is
minimal.

Silent Mind

6.

The more you talk and think,
The more you deviate from the Tao.

Return to silence,
And understanding manifests.

Words are a limitation; they can't describe the formless Reality.

Dream World

7.

Return to the source,
And accord with the Tao.

Engage in worldly pursuits
And you lose your way.

As soon as you perceive the truth,
The world is rightly understood.

Taking appearances for reality
Denotes ignorance.

No need to search for truth;
Only cease to cherish opinions.

Don't hold onto relative views;
Avoid pursuing them.

L OOK TO THE SOURCE, not the manifestations; hold attention on what is permanent—the ultimate Reality, which doesn't come and go—rather than on the ephemeral world which will disappear when you close your eyes for the last time. And when you've come to recognize the false as the false, you need not search for truth.

Three alternate translations rephrase the preceding couplets:

> Go back to the source, and you are One with it.
> Go the way of the world, and you lose the Way.
>
> *
>
> As soon as you know the Truth,
> you will see the world for what it is.
>
> *
>
> The moment you start discriminating
> and preferring, you miss the mark.

Not two, nor one

8.

If you choose between right and wrong,
Confusion enters and Tao is lost.

Duality is the "appearance" of nonduality,
But don't be attached even to nonduality.

A s the Hsin Hsin Ming's verses continue insistently, the nondual teachings are able to develop subtly.

Where the divisive thought process of the dualistic perspective is in operation, we establish a definitive counterpoint for each item that we identify. We envisage the "many"—the pluralistic, material objects—as counterposed to singularity, the "one." In this typically relative construction, each category is a distinct, separate end of a polarity.

Thus, we carry this dualistic propensity into a consideration of the nondual precepts. We notice the "relative" (the countless manifested forms of objects) juxtaposed, in the scriptures, to the "Absolute" (the unformed non-entity which is described as infinite) and we cognize these as independent existences.

But what the nondual sutras are telling us, about such a construction, is that the infinite, all-inclusive reality which is designated Absolute has no opposites. If it were opposite the relative, it would itself be in a relationship to a comparable, limited form. But by the nature of its definition, all limited forms must appear in this field or ground which is not itself simply another limited form. The very word *Absolute* means "unlimited."

And being unlimited and without the restrictions of form, it is freely present across any boundaries of space or time. The Vedas summarize this nondual precept in four words: nowhere is It not.

So, not only has the enlightened sage transcended such polarized conceptions as "good" and "bad," but also the notion that the relative exists on the one hand, while the Absolute exists on the other.

To the author of the Hsin Hsin Ming, the relative is merely an aspect or "appearance" of the one inseparable Reality (or Absolute). But: do not suppose that the Absolute has some sort of existence which is independent of all else that it is; it is not a state, condition or entity in its own right. As the sutras say of it: "Not two, not one." In truth, the Absolute cannot even be conceptualized as the "one thing."

Hence, four translations hinge on this seemingly paradoxical matter:

> All dualities arise from the One;
> but do not be attached even to this "One."
>
>   *
>
> When you assert that things are "real,"
>   you miss their true Reality.
> But to assert that things are "void,"
>   also misses total reality.
>
>   *
>
> Don't get entangled in the "worldly,"
> nor lose yourself in "emptiness."
>
>   *
>
> At the moment of inner enlightenment,
> there is a going beyond "appearance" and
> "emptiness."

No self, no mind

9.

When the mind is at peace,
The phenomenal world does not disturb it.

When the phenomenal world causes no disturbance,
It is as if there is no "world."

When the mind is at peace,
It is as if there is no "mind."

When "agitation" ceases, the mind is quiet.
When the mind becomes quiet, agitation ceases.

"Things" exist because of the mind.
The "mind" exists because of things.

The relativity of the two
Is born of their oneness.

In suchness, the two are one;
And all things are contained in each.

If you do not discriminate,
How can a dualistic view arise?

The Tao is all-embracing.
The Way is neither "easy" nor "difficult".

THERE IS NEITHER WORLD nor self nor mind, from the standpoint of Absolute awareness: all "things" are merely aspects of the one Reality, to which we have assigned descriptive identifications. Let go of all the names and you have Oneness.

Is there ever a thinker who somehow is apart from her thought; is there ever a thought which is apart from a thinker? Is any doer isolated from what is done? Is there a "self" except as by comparison with "others"; does "others" have any meaning except to a "self"? When all such categorical designations are abandoned, the empty mind presides. This is a mind which does not subscribe to "thingness"; it is a mind which will not engender a misleading concept regarding the Absolute.

Three alternate translations speak to the above verses:

> When the mind is still,
> nothing can disturb it.
> When nothing can disturb it,
> reality ceases to exist in the old way.
>
> ⁕
>
> Relinquish separate existences,
> and mind too vanishes.
> When the thinking subject vanishes,
> so too do the objects.
>
> ⁕
>
> Giving rise to "self" generates "others";
> the arising of others gives rise to self.

A noticed condition appears on the screen of consciousness, and we designate it "fear," or "agitation" or some other state. Why not merely be present with whatever is present, without attaching a particular label to it; it just is what it is.

By the time you have named a perceived state, it is already a fact. You will not change what is a fact; you can only either respond to the situation, or react to it. What better response than passive objectivity, recognizing that all impermanent conditions are subject to change? With this response, one's awareness remains undisturbed. In a quiet mind, agitation ceases without effort.

From the standpoint of nondual awareness, a distinctly separate "mind" is not even a reality, nor is there a "self" who is attached to it. As the Sixth Chinese Patriarch, Hui Neng, said in the last couplet of a poem:

> If there is nothing from the start,
> where can the dust alight?

When awareness reverts to its source, the Void, not anything ultimately matters: "the phenomenal world does not disturb it."

Some alternate phrasings apply here, as well:

> Understand the relativity of "two";
> and the basic Reality—the unity of emptiness.
>
> A waste of time, choosing between coarse and fine,
> since Mind gives birth to all things.
>
> Remaining in duality,
> you'll never know unity.

Not to know this unity
lets conflict lead you far astray.

Namelessness

10.

Vacillating in duality leads nowhere.
Attachment leads to division.

You are sure to go astray.
Relax and let things go as they may.

The Tao remains unmoving.

Rest in the Tao and witness the flow,
Easy-going and free from care.

When you hold onto your beliefs,
You turn away from the truth, and fall into confusion.

When your thinking is unsound, you become troubled;
So what is the value of one-sided views?

ALL EARTHLY PHENOMENA COME AND GO within a constant Reality that does not—being eternal, which means "without beginning or end"—come or go. "The true purpose of Zen," said Shunryu Suzuki Roshi, "is to see things as they are [objectively], and to let everything go as it goes." In Taoism, this non-resistance is known as the "watercourse" way. It is to have no predilection for how things "ought" to go, as opposed to how they are going.

Contrast this attitude with what is considered to be "idealism." We conceive some idea, for example, as to how we ought to behave, some ideal standard to which we compare our ensuing behavior (e.g., "What would Jesus do?"). As a consequence, we forever find ourself falling short of our idealistic—and unrealistic—criterion. This leads to dissatisfaction, discontent, and particularly to self-critique. And the same ideal standard to which we compare ourself is the same standard we use to compare others. Meanwhile, obviously, each of us is doing precisely what we are capable of doing and inclined to do—or else we would actually be doing something else.

In the freed and empty mind, there are no such ideas, ideals, opinions or judgments, nor belief in the virtue of rigid and limited standards. One's behavior is spontaneous, unpremeditated, unconstrained by notions of "rightness."

The empty mind is free of "gaining ideas," such as the presumption that "I will be a better person, if only..." this or that were the case. This even applies to enlightenment. If we assume that we will be a better person if enlightened, we are consciously moving away from the ultimate Reality which is ever-present right here, right now—the very same ultimate Reality which we hope that enlightenment will lead us to. This is what in Buddhism is called "grasping at the wind." Enlightenment is merely the name for a condition of namelessness, emptiness, non-grasping.

Alternative translations apply to the verses above:

> Accept the wisdom of not naming things,
> and rest in the silence of Being.
>
> •
>
> Just let things be,
> for all is exactly as it should be.
>
> •
>
> Even to be attached to the idea of "enlightenment"
> is to go astray.
>
> •
>
> Obeying our nature, we're in accord—
> wandering freely, without annoyance.

Come what may

11.

If you want to be in accord with the Tao,
Don't deny the phenomenal world.

When you recognize the source of the senses,
You are open to enlightened perception.

The wise are passive.
The foolish tie themselves in knots:

Though the truth is undivided,
They become attached to particular things.

To try to catch the wind with the hand
Is a grave error.

The foolish vacillate between
Having and not having.

The wise show no preferences.

A S LONG AS YOUR PHYSICAL ORGANISM continues to survive, you are a subject of this relative, material world. The body has a relationship to its immediate needs and to the environment in which it functions. Whether enlightened or not, we continue to experience Reality through the medium of our senses; and this world of matter is an element of that experience. The "six senses"* too are It, not remote from the objects sensed as It.

For the awakened, whatever experience that the body, senses or mind encounters is okay: it must be okay, because it happens to be "what is." So, the sage does not avoid—nor seek out—any particular bodily experience: whatever presents is a manifestation of That.

This means (and this is a difficult precept for people to grasp) that even when what presents to the mind or body is not okay, that too—the not-okayness—is still okay. There's no law in the universe that says you have to like everything which appears on the screen of consciousness or as a bodily sensation. But, your not "liking" it too is That doing what it does—presenting as actuality, Reality, "as it is."

Here's how one of the alternate translations puts it:

> If you want to know the One...
> Allow your senses what comes your way;
> but don't be entangled in what comes.

---

* Buddhism adds consciousness, as a sense, to sight, hearing, smell, taste and touch.

The last two of the three verses, given before (Chapter 11), are interpreted in several meaningful ways in the alternative translations. "The wise are passive" is also rendered as "take things as they come"; "take no special action"; "have no motives." And, following are five more interpretations:

> The wise do not strive after goals;
> but fools put themselves in bondage.

> The wise do not strive—
> Though the truth is One,
> the fool clings to "this" and "that."

> The wise person acts without emotion;
>   he knows all things are the One.
> The ignorant person sees
>   differences everywhere.

> The ignorant are bound to emotions.
> The wise one reacts not at all.

> Those who know most, do least.
> Wisdom neither loves nor hates.

Equanimity

12.

Delusions arise from the thinking mind:
Why treat the creations of the mind
As though they are concretely real?

The mind goes to extremes;
Let go of extremes, and return to equanimity.

When the eyes are wide open,
The dreams cease.

When the mind abides in nonduality,
All things display their true nature.

When this essence is fathomed,
Attachments cease.

When all things are perceived in their oneness,
The source is seen to have never been apart.

Distinctions and divisions end.

These four verses can not be better summarized than by alternate translations:

No comparisons are possible
in the relationless state.

All things seen equally,
the timeless essence is reached.

Seen without differentiation,
the One is everywhere revealed.

If you would understand dualities,
know that they spring from the Absolute void.
The Absolute and all dualities are one,
and from it all things originate.

Undivided

13.

Objects appear to move,
Relative to objects at rest.

Objects appear to be at rest,
Relative to objects in motion.

When nonduality is perceived,
Even the concept of oneness is dissolved.

The Tao is not bound by rules and measures:
The mind in accord with it
Abides in tranquil space.

Doubts and confusions cease.

Belief is dissolved by understanding.
Bondage to things and ideas has ceased.

All is effortlessly empty and clear;
Seeking and separating don't intrude here.

Here, there is neither self nor other;
Subject and object are one.

CONFUSION CEASES WITH ENLIGHTENMENT; doubts, opinions and beliefs end. What does any person need to "believe" in: Reality is ever-present and self-evident. When conceptions about it are released, there is no estrangement from It.

With concepts absent, even the idea of "holiness" is dismissed. Hence, in Buddhism (where many strive to become a buddha) there is an expression, "If you see Buddha on the road, kill him."

With these deep shifts in perception, one's values change; and, consequently one's behavior changes. When neither "self" nor "other" are viewed as separate entities, one's behavior changes. No longer concerned with self-improvement, and thus self-importance, one's behavior changes perceptibly.

Three alternate translations provide assurances:

> This is the One
> to which all things return.
> All things are within the One,
> there is no outside.
>
> *
>
> Realize the mystery of One-essence
> and be released from entanglements.
>
> *
>
> When you no longer are asleep
> all dreams will vanish by themselves.

The "oneness" of the ubiquitous Infinite is not a joining of two, or more, distinctive things. It is the absence of "thingness": "There is nothing from the start."

A "you" and an "I" do not join together to form some third condition, such as "unity." Where the "you" and the "I" disappear, there is automatic consubstantiality: it was the fact even before the "you" and the "I" were conceptualized.

So there need be no goal of "unification," only a relinquishing of the dualistic perspective. Acknowledge that which permeates all, and unity is present. As a couple of translations put it:

> Free of description,
> all is an undivided whole.

> For the mind in unity,
> "individual" activity ceases.

The "individual" itself, sensed as who you think you are, disappears into the Void. No longer a separate "person"—with, as is said in Buddhism, "nothing left to stand on"—there is freedom from attachment to the push and pull of relative conditions. Action now is without concern for outcome, and without fear of the world's disregard for one's self-interests. "You are not the doer," as the sutras say.

> In this Emptiness,
> both "self" and "other" are no more.

> If you don't perpetuate duality,
> how can even [your] identity remain?

For the realized mind,
self-centered striving ceases.

You are free
when there's nothing left
to hold onto.

All-encompassing

14.

All things are of this suchness, not one thing is excluded.
The wise all share this understanding.

Transcending the concepts of time and space,
The moment is eternal.

And in it,
The Tao is manifest everywhere.

To exclude any aspect of Reality is obviously dualistic. The enlightened sage does not go halfway in the Way. Consistency, integrity, honesty are markers of the open path; and the recognition "all is That, doing what it does" is applied to both negative and positive circumstances without equivocation.

The infinitely Boundless encompasses all that "is" or "is not," that which "has been" and "will be," that which is "here" and "there" and their interface, whatever is viewed as good, bad or indifferent.

All is the same, all is undivided, in Absolute awareness; this is the condition in which the awakened one's perception abides; this is the clarity in which one lives out the remainder of earthly life. Even the "Absolute" vanishes, in this empty awareness, without even an effort to "purify" the mind.

Six alternate phrasings follow:

"Not two" includes everything,
excludes nothing.

*

This is the space that always exists
and that holds all within.

*

"Here" and "not here" don't apply.
Everywhere, It is right before your eyes.

*

This is where thinking never attains
and where imagination fails to measure.

When dualism does no longer obtain,
even "oneness" itself remains not as such.

The enlightened of all times and places
have entered into this Truth.

Timeless

15.

Small is small, only relative to large.
Distinction being relative,

Distinction is unimportant
When duality is forsaken.

In the Absolute,
"What is" and "what is not" are the same.

Don't abide in what seems otherwise.

WHERE NO SEPARATE FORMS are conceived, even "existence" and "non-existence" are devoid of meaning. The Absolute is not dependent upon the categories of existence or non-existence, being timeless.

Where no distinctive conditions are conceived, "enlightenment" and "vexation" have no definite relevance. Therefore, it should be clear that time, in relation to a goal, is not a factor in discerning Reality. Nor are any doctrines necessary.

Where there is no fragmentation, there are no obstacles. Where there are no obstructions, there are no conflicts. Even if conflict was present, that too would be a manifestation of Reality. A disciple asked a Zen master, who was terminally ill, about the current state of his health; the sage replied, "Sun-faced Buddha, moon-faced Buddha!"

Your original mind was an empty mind. In it, not anything ever really mattered. And you and the Absolute were One, in that condition, without either "you" or the "One" existing.

Even what's written here are idle words; no need for you to retain them. Reality will be the same whether you "do" or "do not"; whatever "you" do is Reality.

If you do not awaken to this truth,
do not worry yourself about it.

＊

Whether you see It or not
is of no consequence.

Essence

16.

The all contains each,
And each is the essence of the all.

To live in this understanding
Is the essence of Tao.

The understanding mind
Is undivided.

No explanation is needed
Where there is no "mind."

Three more alternate translations bring us back full-circle, without need now for commentary:

> Delusion breeds the concepts "tranquil"
> and "disordered."
> Enlightenment tells you
> there's no good or bad.
>
> Each thing reveals the One;
> the One manifests as all things.
>
> Take your stand on this,
> and the rest will follow inseparably.

The Tao is self-evident
To those who live in choiceless awareness.

When you perceive everything objectively,
Your path is clear and unobstructed.

Addenda

I. THE OXHERDING PICTURES

Another revered Zen teaching tool, the Ten Oxherding Pictures are attributed to a 12th-century Chinese Zen master Kuo-an Shih-yuan (Kakuan Shien, to the Japanese). The pictures are said to have been created as a vehicle to teach Zen to the illiterate, but all ten are accompanied with both a prose and a poem explication. A brush-painting illustration of each picture, by Gyokusei Jikihara, is available—along with an English translation of the wording—in *Three Pillars of Zen*, a Buddhist primer of the Zen master Phillip Kapleau. A more-detailed line-drawing version can be found in Arthur Braverman's *Warrior of Zen*, created by his wife Hiroko.

The series begins with the central figure, a young man, "seeking the Ox," which in general is a figurative form for the Absolute (or an enlightened perspective on it). Though he has a bridle rope in hand, thinking he knows what he'll encounter, the first prose sentence admonishes: "The Ox has never really gone astray, so why search for it?" The poetic version tells us, "At evening, he hears cicadas chirping in the trees." The Absolute not only is ever-present, but he has already encountered a form of it through his sense of hearing.

In picture two, he has come across "tracks" of the Ox: "Through the sutras and teachings," this seeker has been apprised that "each and every thing is a manifestation" of what he's looking for. The poem points out how omnipresent this ultimate reality is: "Even the deepest gorges, of the topmost mountains, can't hide this Ox's nose—which reaches right to heaven."

Picture three, the Ox is within his sense of sight; in fact, even his senses themselves are It. "The six senses are no different from this true Source. In every activity [even the seeker's animation], the Source is manifestly present.... [even] that which is seen is identical with the true Source." The poem adds: "A nightingale warbles on a twig, the sun shines on undulating willows. There stands the Ox—where could it hide?"

In the fourth picture, the Ox is apprehended. He and the Ox (having been "grasped") are one connected unit. What will his progress be, now that both arms are around the Ox?

In picture five, he and the Ox can now move together, but there are still changes to unfold in how he lives his (now goal-less) life. He notices, for example, that what before were considered troublesome thoughts, "even they arise from our True nature."

Picture six: the Ox is now carrying him wherever he goes. Such dualistic ideas as "gain and loss no longer affect him.... in his heart, profound tranquility prevails."

7. "Ox forgotten," he no longer even thinks of himself as a "Buddhist" or an "enlightened" being. "In this dharma, there is no twoness."

8. "Self forgotten," all is now viewed merely as the One: self, others—both identities are recognized to be mere concepts, ideas about things.

9. His relationship to the world at large is one of openness and non-resistance. Neither the sacred nor the profane are differently valued. "He observes the waxing and waning of life in the world, while abiding unassertively in a state of unshakeable serenity."

The tenth picture shows a man, now years older, who is once again to be found in the village marketplace. A simple figure, "barechested, barefooted he comes into the marketplace." Through his example alone, "he leads innkeepers and fishmongers in the Way of the Buddha." His presence changes lives without even an intention to do so. "Without recourse to mystic powers, withered trees he swiftly brings to bloom."

II. ENLIGHTENMENT POETRY

The Chinese Zen master Sheng Yen compiled, two decades ago, ten poems that were composed by Buddhist teachers in China during past centuries, *The Poetry of Enlightenment*. Among these English translations is the Hsin Hsin Ming; and the others, like it, reflect a similar spirit in the transmission of the teachings. Examples follow:

Shih Wang
Ming
(6th c.)

Not dying, not born,
Without form or name,
The Tao is empty and tranquil.
The myriad phenomena are equal.

* * *

Fu Wu
(d. 569)

When the nature of mind departs
    from emptiness,
It can be sacred *or profane*.

* * *

Shih
T'ou
(d. 790)

Moving forward there is no near or far;
Confusion creates mountains and rivers of
    obstructions.
I implore those who investigate the mysterious:
Do not waste your time!

Niu T'ou
(d. 657)
Mind is without alienation;
No need to terminate lust.

●

In one-mindedness there are no
    wandering thoughts,
The myriad conditions harmonize.

●

When in confusion, you must discard affairs;
Enlightened, it makes no difference.

●

Completely penetrating everything,
It has always pervaded everywhere.

●●●

Yung
Chia
(d. 713)
Put down the four elements, don't cling to anything;
In this Nirvanic nature, feel free to eat and drink.
All phenomena are impermanent; all are empty.
This is the complete enlightenment of the Tathagata.

●

Walking is Ch'an; sitting is Ch'an;
Speaking or silent, moving or still, the essence is
    undisturbed.
Remain composed even if facing a sharp weapon,
Be at ease even if given poison.

●

It is not perishable and cannot be praised,
Its substance is like limitless space.
Without leaving where it is, it is constantly clear.
When seeking, you know it cannot be found.
It cannot be grasped, nor can it be discarded;
It is obtained only in the unobtainable.

*　*　*

Tung Shan
(d. 869)

As before a precious mirror,
The form and reflection gaze on each other—
You are not it,
But it is just you.

*

Natural and subtle,
It is neither ignorance nor enlightenment.

*　*　*

Hanshan
Te Ch'ing
(d. 1623)

Thus perfected ones
First empty the defilement of self.
When the defilement of self is emptied
How can the outer realm be an obstruction?

*

Resilience is the function
Of the self forgotten.
As soon as idiosyncrasies appear
You recognize them immediately.

*

Look upon the body as unreal,
An image in a mirror, the reflection of the
    moon in water.
Contemplate the mind as formless,
Yet bright and pure.

*

If nothing arises within the mind,
Nothing will manifest without.
That which has characteristics
Is not original reality.

A further sampling of enlightenment poetry over the ages,
reflecting the spirit of the Hsin Hsin Ming:

Dao de jing
(c. 500 B.C.)

Once the whole is divided,
the parts need names.
There are already enough names.
One must know when to stop.

∗

In the pursuit of learning,
every day something is acquired.
In the pursuit of Tao,
every day something is dropped.

∗

To die
but not to perish
is to be eternally present.

∗

All those will come to him
who keeps to the One;
for there lies rest,
and happiness, and peace.

∗∗∗

Confucius
(d. 479 B.C.)

One who sees the Way
in the morning
can gladly die
in the evening.

∗∗∗

88

Hui Neng
(d. 713)

For the person with correct views,
the Buddha will call at your home.

◦ ◦ ◦

the
awakened
Dogen
Kigen
Zenji
(d. 1253)

For many years, snow has covered
    the mountain.
This year the snow *is* the mountain.

◦ ◦ ◦

Dogen
Zenji

No wind,
no waves,
the empty boat
is flooded with moonlight.

◦

Attaining this way,
one's daily life
is the realization
of ultimate reality.

◦ ◦ ◦

Zen
master
Wumen
Huikai
(d. 1260)

Gautama Buddha acted
    shamelessly...
Hanging out mutton,
he sold dog meat
as if it were so wonderful!

◦ ◦ ◦

Zen
master
Jakushitsu

The good news
should not be spread
frivolously.
That valley stream and mountain
beyond those eaves
talk too much.

I hate the sound
of the word Buddha.
I have little regard
for Zen of the patriarchs.
None of the many dharmas
touches my heart.
I simply face the green mountain,
pillow puffed high,
and nap.

Ikkyū,
resigning
as an
abbot
(1440)

Ten days in this temple
and my mind is reeling!
Between my legs
the red thread [arousal]
stretches and stretches:
If you come some other day
asking for me,
better look in a fish stall,
a saki shop, or a brothel.

Ikkyū

In this world,
all things
without exception
are unreal.
Death itself
is an illusion.

A single moon
bright and clear
in an unclouded sky—
yet still we stumble
in the world's darkness.

Writing something
to leave behind
is yet another kind of dream.
When *I awake*,
I know that there will be
no one to read it.

● ● ●

Zen
master
Bunan
(d. 1676)

Die while alive,
be completely dead!
Then do what you will
and all will be well.

● ● ●

Samurai
Miyamoto
Mushashi

While on the Way,
do not begrudge death.

91

***

Hakuin
(d. 1769)

The cause of our sorrow
is ego delusion.

*

Our form *now* being no-form,
in "going" and "returning"
we never leave Home.

***

Ryōkan,
c. 1800

Can I last
until spring finally arrives?
Unable to beg for rice,
how will I survive the chill?
Even meditation helps no longer.

***

Sodo
Yokayama,
Roshi

The Sea of Midway Island
doesn't know of my brother's death.
My brother
doesn't know either.

***

Sogaku
Harada,
Roshi
(d. 1961)

For forty years
I've been selling water
by the bank of a river.

III. Sheng Yen

Following are a few comments that have been made by Sheng Yen, a contemporary Zen teacher (from *Faith in Mind*):

❊

Everything is absolute in the sense that there is no separation between you and others, between past and future.

❊

Great space does not refer to a nothingness, but rather to a totality. Though It includes everything, there is no individual existence.

❊

Holding on to various likes and dislikes keeps you apart from the Way. Discarding them will bring you in accord with the Way.

❊

If you take an equal attitude towards everything, all differences will disappear, along with existence itself.

❊

Liberation goes beyond both emptiness and form.

❊

Everything is generated by the one and will eventually return to the one. This concept can be found in both oriental and western philosophy. But in Buddha Dharma even that state is not good enough.

Buddha nature is the totality of your own self. Why should it be necessary to try to attain it?

The state of one can only be considered in relation to two. A true totality would not even be considered "one"; it can only be called "nothing." It is only when a distinction is made that the one can exist at all, and in that case it will lead to two. You can only feel lonely when you are aware of the possible existence of another person. In complete totality, there is no sense of loneliness.

IV. DENNIS GENPO MERZEL

A number of comments by American Zen master Dennis Genpo Merzel, author of *The Eye Never Sleeps,* are pertinent here:

The Way refers to the Tao, the order of the universe. The Tao, the Way as it is, before the mind interferes, is in perfect order; the Tao is just 'what it is.'

When we talk about Truth with a capital T, meaning the absolute Truth, then there can be only one Truth, only one Way; and that one Way can be found in all religions and practices.

With that one Truth, there is no division between knower and known, subject and object; there is just the One, your true nature, your real self.

❀

The key point here is to cease seeing things in a dualistic way, to free ourselves from dualistic ideas and ultimately from dualistic consciousness itself.

❀

We bind ourselves. How? The very act of definition itself creates a boundary.

❀

When two people are together without boundary, there is no object, so the subject also disappears; and vice versa, with no subject, the object disappears. That is called One Mind. That is true transmission.

❀

If there is even the thought that he or she is not me, if there is even the idea that the tree and I are separate, then dualistic thinking arises and confusion happens.

❀

If we are all made of the same essence, if everything arises from a single source, then everything is nothing but this one essence, through and through.

❀

In the absence of discriminating thoughts, the "mind" as we know it ceases to exist. Our suffering—our feeling of discomfort, alienation, loneliness—arises because we create a dualistic way of perceiving everything, that separates us from the external.

❀

Out of this comes the concept that I exist as a separate entity apart from the whole: there is a me in the world, looking out at the world. This concept of a separate self is the fragmentation.

❀

Fear is guarding the doorway to reality, fear of stepping off the hundred-foot pole, of letting go of who we think we are, of what we cherish, of our identity. Whatever we identify with has to be dropped.

❀

When you let go and stop clinging to your own opinions, ideas, and preferences, then you realize the one Truth, absolute reality, the One that can never change.

❀

The basic fear is, "Who would I be without my opinions and notions?" That's the point! You wouldn't be. You would cease to exist in the old way.

❀

When you cut off this dualistic mind, all your aversions and preferences, then you become one with your life, one with the Way. Therefore, as attachments arise, don't take a position for or against them. Just notice them. Just be aware. That is the key word: aware.

When you empty yourself of all opinions, notions, concepts, and ideas of self; when you become thoroughly void of ego; when you sit here as zero, as nothing; then what comes out of your heart is the true Dharma.

When we stop holding on to our likes and dislikes, our attachment and aversion toward everything and everyone, then the mind as we now know it ceases to exist. This is what is called dropping the mind or forgetting the self. When we forget the self, then any object in the external world ceases to exist in the familiar way, as a separate object outside ourselves. Then all objects are no other than ourselves: the mountains, the trees, the rocks, the grasses, the blue sky, the moon, everything— all One Mind, Buddha Mind. Everything in existence, all that arises, not only material objects but also thoughts and emotions, is nothing but Mind, nothing but the Buddhadharma. We can call it God or the source or one's true nature. Whatever name we give it, it is all One.

The very effort to stop the ceaseless movement of thoughts keeps us stirred up. Just give up all this effort to stop thinking!

What do we mean by nonthinking? Simply allowing thoughts to bubble up into the mind and pass away is nonthinking. Nonthinking is that which goes beyond either thoughts or no thoughts: it is neither blank mind nor busy mind. When the mind is allowed to rest naturally, there is no problem.

*

Once we realize the Way, it is not limited to sitting; everything we do from morning to night is nothing but the Way. But until we realize this Way, nothing we do is really the Way.

*

An awakened one is not a person who merely has had some kind of experience and then goes on to live his or her life unconsciously, insensitively, inattentively.

*

Our perspective shifts, it is no longer stuck in a fixed egocentric position.

*

Our nature is no-nature. Our true self is no-self. Our true mind is no-mind. Our true essence of mind is no-essence, no-thingness.

*

When you truly lose everything, you gain everything, which is absolutely nothing.

*

After all, both delusion and enlightenment are only concepts. There is no delusion and no enlightenment. One who realizes this completely, with the whole being, is called "enlightened."

＊

We must avoid clinging to the experience of enlightenment, the realization of being it. It flows through me; I am just a conduit.

＊

When you jump like that, the only thing you ever lose is your personal identity, your ego. What you find is your true life, your real life, the one that has no limit, the one that does not feel constricted and confined. What you find is tremendous space, freedom, liberation, peace.

V. SUZUKI ROSHI ON THE SANDOKAI
Relevant comments of Suzuki Roshi, in speaking of a Zen poem/treatise, the Sandokai, similar to the Hsin Hsin Ming:

＊

If we think, "I am here and the mountain is over there," that is a dualistic way of observing things. . . . So, our [Buddhist] understanding is that there is one whole Being that includes everything, and that the "many things" are found in one whole being. . . . "Many" and "one" are different ways of describing one whole being. . . . they are originally one.

＊

Whatever happens to us, we are not bothered. . . . It is like something happening in the great sky. Whatever kind of bird flies through it, the sky doesn't care. . . . You may think of something, but your mind doesn't care.

＊

In this sense, all things have equal, absolute value. ...
and thus is equal to everything else.... The mountain
is not more valuable because it is "high"; the river is not
less valuable because it is "low".... The absolute is the
absolute because it is beyond our intellectual or dualistic
thinking.

VI. A Few Offerings

Reviewing all these verses, I'm challenged to respond with
a few offerings of my own:

> Mired in duality,
> I choose
> my shoes:
> wear
> the Good Pair
> or the Bad Pair?

> everything emptied
> out of the bucket,
> there is something
> which cannot be emptied.
> what is that?

> He is proud
> to be practical;
> she is pleased
> to be unemotional:
> both are limited
> by their own
> definitions.

> We are a zero,
> trying to become a one;

And so we are neither a complete zero
nor an entire one.

⁕

To be living your life
in such a way
that there's nothing you'd do tomorrow
which you're not doing today...

⁕

The human mind
is limited.
Filled with knowledge,
where is there room
for truth?

⁕

It all means nothing!
Even the moon
is a big goose egg
in the sky.
It all means nothing—
and that's the
exciting part!

⁕

groping
in the dark
for the light switch:
once found,
no longer needed

⁕⁕⁕

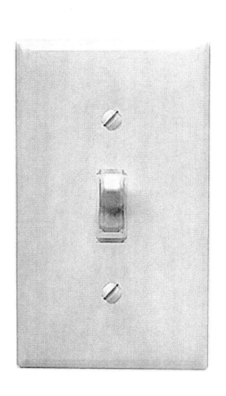

In Death as in Life*

    I had no way of knowing, when I set out, that I would be the last of the disciples of the Tathagata, as he was called – "the transcendent one."

    He and his group of attendants had left Pava and were on their way toward Kusinara, having gone afoot at daybreak. Knowing that he would appear before an assembled gathering in that village, I'd hoped to catch up with them while they tarried there. I'd had a restless night, contemplating the implications of his message after dinner in Pava, and had hoped to ask him my question before they departed from there. But after lying awake much of the night, I fell asleep before daybreak and awoke with the sun in my eyes.

    They, mostly being older, would have a slower gait than I, so I was confident that – setting out right away – I would overtake them in time. So, I was surprised, when I was about half way on the dusty road from Pava, to come down over a rise and see the knot of his robed followers tightly gathered in the shade between two sal trees, a shouting distance away. They were unaware of my approach, the dozen or so of them huddled around and leaning over what was in their midst, and the few voices to be heard were muffled. A couple of them sat on their

* Based on a true story, circa 483 BC.

105

haunches – their water bags nearby, off their shoulders – and the one facing me looked up protectively as I drew near. He held up his hand, signaling me to halt. He said something to the others, some of whom turned to look at me, and he rose and came over. Where he had been, I could see – in the light between the men's legs – a figure at their feet. The master? Had he been hurt? A viper bite?

I recognized the disciple as he drew near, the one with the long, thin face; I'd heard him called Yasa. He looked perturbed, but nodded in greeting:

"Hello, friend. You left the road. Do you mean to be of help?"

"Your master," I stammered. "I've been hoping to ask a question of your master."

"Ah, then. I see." His countenance cleared. "Not possible right now." He shook his head.

Impulsively I asked: "Is he injured?"

"No. Ill."

"What is it? Do you know?"

"Not certain yet."

We heard a groan, then vomiting. Yasa glanced anxiously over his shoulder, then turned to leave.

I called, "I'll wait nearby. In case I can be of help."

Without acknowledging me, Yasa melted back into the group. A pitched voice could be heard giving directions. Two men moved away, stringing a rope between the two trees. A wide cotton cloth was thrown over the rope. Rocks were moved into place to hold the shelter's corners down. Bed rolls were unfurled. The mass of perhaps as many as twenty bodies were maneuvering as a unit, apparently moving their master's prostrate form into the enclosure. From where I sat, on a flat rock under a pipal tree, I could see just the backs of grey robes waving in deep shadow, and the plane of dun cloth above a few of the bobbing, shaved heads.

It felt good to sit in the shade. The sun was at its zenith, this day in May. Feeling hunger now, I drank from my water pouch and chewed on some betel leaves. Several of the disciples were sitting now, facing the enclosure. One soon rose, nodded to something being said, and he headed toward the road. As he came near where I was sitting, I recognized him: Achitanaya, Cunda's son. I held up my hand in greeting; he shaded his eyes and looked in my direction, then came over.

"Subhadda!" He seemed surprised. "Why are you here?"

"I have a question to ask your master. But Yasa told me that he is ill. Can I be of help?"

"Not yet. I'm hurrying back to Pava, to bring Benai the herbalist. The master is weak, has a fever and stomach pains. He is resting, and Ananda is by his side. I must go!"

I nodded. "I'll be waiting here."

As I watched Achit ascend the dusty road, I fell into contemplation, with some images of past events appearing before the mind's eye.

●●●

It was about a year ago when I had heard, from someone passing by my hermitage, that Achitanaya was leaving Pava, to join the Tathagata and his mendicants when they were rumored to arrive in Vesali. When Achit came back to Pava, a couple of months ago, for a visit with his family, he told me about the master and his teachings; and – challenging to me as an ascetic – how the master had transcended self-limitation after abandoning all purifying austerities. Achit also told his father about the Tathagata's ability to show seekers the face of Brahman; and so Cunda, the goldsmith, gave Achit a full purse as a gift for the sangha and asked that he beg the teacher to visit Pava. I, too, expressed to Achit my desire to hear the teacher's words firsthand, though I could give no gift.

107

So, leaving again to return to his master, Achitanaya learned they had gone to Beluva; and, there, he did ask the master to favor Pava with his presence. When the group arrived at Pava's park, Achit summoned all of his family and their many friends, and sent someone to call me from my hermitage. Curious villagers began to gather around us, as well.

It was late afternoon. Achit explained to us, as the master sat among his resting attendants, that it was the sangha's practice – when entering a village after trekking all day – to go house-to-house with their rice bowls, accepting offerings of food. After they had received enough for all of the group to share, they – and those villagers who were curious to hear what message he brought – would sit at the master's feet and enjoy his presence.

Cunda was impatient to hear what the transcendent one could impart. He told Achitanaya to lead the group to his home; he could provide enough food for all. And so, everyone followed Achit to his father's manse, with the mendicants by his side.

In scarcely an hour, Cunda had a feast prepared (his whole family following his orders) while the mendicants sat quietly in the courtyard, around their master, the group appearing to be in deep contemplation. Achit, meanwhile, called me over to the main entrance: the villagers who were at the park had gone home to tell their families that Cunda was preparing a feast; there would not be enough food for both the sangha and the curious villagers, so he was going to close the outer gate. He wanted me to watch over the room and tell anyone, who might try to enter, why the gate had been closed. When he saw my hesitance, he said in assurance that the Tathagata would return to Pava in two days, after a visit to Kusinara, and would appear before the villagers, at the park. So, I agreed to act as sentinel.

From my position at one end of the main room, I was able to observe the mendicants' entry from the courtyard. They moved so fluidly, as a group, that it was difficult to be sure of their number. And it took me a few moments to conclude which of them was the Tathagata: Achitanaya had told me that the master was eighty years old, but that two of the disciples were yet older. Only by the deference of the others, to the one who seemed least noticeable, was I able to determine their teacher. As soon as they had drawn near the serving table, Cunda loudly addressed everyone. My eyes were on the teacher. The group's eyes were on the food, but they looked up respectfully when Cunda spoke. Except for the teacher: his eyes were fixed on one of the two dozen bowls of food.

Cunda boasted, as usual: his was the good fortune, he said, to host the Tathagata and his monks; Brahma had rewarded him with success in his trade because of his sacrifices and devotion. Tonight, he was expressing his gratitude for the visit of the transcendent one; and each of the different dishes offered was prepared separately, with his personal supervision. He himself, in anticipation of this honor, had harvested herbs, foraged mushrooms, and selected the vegetables. After the guests could enjoy his humble offering (he finally concluded), he would be blessed with any words of advice they might bestow.

The monks bowed in gratitude. Achitanaya bowed to the Tathagata and indicated that he choose the first dish. The master bowed to his disciple, now his host, and chose the mushroom dish that he had been regarding. The others each followed with their choice of dish; warm chapatis were given to each by Cunda's wife; and the group sat together in a circle, quietly enjoying Cunda's offering.

Cunda's wife asked me to go to the puja room and prepare it. I lit candles, lit incense, took a place near the corner of the room, and waited. Shortly, Cunda and his family lead the guests to the room; the family sat along one wall, Cunda at the forefront; teacher and disciples sat along the opposite wall, the transcendent one toward the middle. Achitanaya sat with his master. The monks lowered their eyes, and remained in silent contemplation until Cunda, growing restless, broke the silence.

"Venerable sadhu, I've heard that you have been in the presence of Brahman. How may a humble servant like myself enjoy such a grace as that?"

The transcendent one looked into Cunda's eyes, and spoke of our lives as unsatisfied, unfulfilled desire; even the hope to know the unknowable. Hopes and ambitions that life renders into disappointment and distress; and out of this distress, a cycle of even greater hopes and desires – pulling us and pushing us, until it all vanishes as quickly as a dream…at the end of our allotted time. When, in the morning, a dream vanishes, do you concern yourself with what the dream figures were intent on accomplishing? Do you go about the day arguing the opinions that these dream figures expressed; or righting the wrongs which were done them? A dream is impermanent, it has no worth; all that is impermanent vanishes in time. Is this body permanent? This mind? This self? What remains when all else comes and goes? Is that present now?

The Tathagata fell silent. All were silent; breathing, and the sputtering of incense, was all that could be heard. After a while Cunda sighed, rose, and lead his family out, after inviting the monks to rest the night in the puja room. Achitanaya gathered their water pouches, and I refilled them at the well, while he went to a storeroom and brought each monk a small cotton bedroll.

I was eager to get out into the night air and the quiet walk back to the hermitage. "What remains when all else comes and goes?" Not the body. Not the mind. Not the self. These are all impermanent. What is permanent? What does not come and go? Is it present now? If I purify myself and overcome my imperfections, I hope to be graced with seeing it face-to-face. Hope to… Hope… desire… unsatisfied… unfulfilled. "Hope to know the unknowable." Disappointment… distress. What is present now, that does not come and go? Why had the Tathagata forsaken austerities? What did he discover when he gave up all hope of self-perfection… self… dream figures… come and go… what doesn't come and go?

"Is that present now?" I endured a restless night. The moon was nearly full. Its phases will come and go like dreams. My practice…fourteen years…his was six years (Achit said) and nearly brought him to death…eating fallen leaves and drinking river water…hoping to be pure enough. "Is that present now?" I was looking at the moon; and then the sun was in my eyes.

* * *

The sun was again in my eyes. I had leaned back against the pipal tree, with eyes closed in contemplation of what had brought me here. The sun had lowered, the shade had passed. Sounds from the road roused me, Achitanaya hurrying past with Benai the herbalist. They pass through the circle of monks; there is murmuring, heads bobbing, movement near the enclosure, collecting of water pouches. A long wait. Benai re-emerges through the group, with Achit, who hands her a small purse. Benai hands it back, shaking her head. Benai hoists her goatskin bag onto her shoulder and heads toward the road, back to Pava. I raise my hand to catch Achit's eye, and he comes over. He reaches into his robe and hands me a dry rice ball. I bow in thanks.

"The illness…?," I query.

Achit slowly shakes his head, as if denying something. "Nothing to be done. Benai could only give some herbs to reduce pain, fever and vomiting." Achit lowers his head, as a tear forms. "Poisoning."

"How can Benai know it's that?!"

"The master knows."

"Mushroom poisoning?," I ask slowly.

"Yes. The master...." He nods.

"That bowl, last night. He had first choice…"

"My father gathered the mushrooms. He never bothered to gather them before. He knows nothing about them!" Achit wiped his eyes.

"You told me your master lived in the forest for six years. He must have known them on sight. Why didn't he tell Cunda?"

"Ha. You know my father. Proud, arrogant. He would have eaten a handful, insulted at having his judgment questioned. Then he would have passed the dish around, bristling if others declined to sample it!" He sobbed, and added. "The master knew." A long pause. Then, with irony, he recalled, "He once said, 'who begs for food, eats what's offered'!" More sobbing.

We were silent. Then I asked, "While the master is alive, could I ask him a question?"

"I don't know. We'll see now." He motioned to me to follow. I left my water pouch and rice ball; we made our way to the ring of disciples, who parted for us. Some were quietly weeping. The one known as Ananda sat outside the cloth enclosure, an old man looking very tired. Achitanaya bent over and said something to him. Ananda looked up sharply at me: "You would disturb the Tathagata? He is very ill, and not inclined to answer a sannyasi's questions now." A guttural voice from the other side of the curtain called out, "Ananda!" Ananda ducked under the curtain. Achit and I turned to leave. Ananda came out from under the curtain, and tugged on Achit's robe: "The Tathagata would like the sannyasi to ask his question." He held up a corner of the curtain, for me to enter.

The faint smell of herbs, and vomit, greeted my nostrils. Waning sunlight lit the back of the enclosure, making it difficult for me to see the features of the master. He was lying on his side, on a thick mat of sal leaves, his head propped up by a couple of bed rolls. His only covering was a jute blanket.

He raised himself on one elbow. I can only remember his eyes: alert like a dog's – impersonal, but attentive. He looked at me silently, searchingly. Did he remember seeing me last night, I wondered. Sensing Ananda would be impatient, I blurted, "You renounced your austerities...?"

A slight smile, as if he were amused. "Sadhu, renounce even renouncing." A pause. "But is that your question?"

I relaxed; my attention focused. "That which doesn't come or go; it's not the self?" I squatted near him.

"Not self. But all selves."

"So, it is this yogi and all yogis?"

"All that is; and all that is not." He raised a finger: "Tathagata, Gautama, sadhu, monk, teacher, master, beggar, fool. Different names for one thing. Why these names? Because no one can know that one thing. Immanent, yes. And transcendent, yes. Being all things, it is unknowable – except to the knower of that: and the knower is just another name for the unknowable. Sadhu, having no separate identity, it is not knowable. It is all that is known, thus all-knowing."

"It is what knows," I ventured. "That is another name for it."

"Present now and always. Permanently impermanent."

He shuddered in a grip of pain, and closed his eyes. He then looked at me again, with a slight smile.

"Existence and non-existence are the same, then?," I asked.

"All things."

"I see no fear in you. Is that why?"

His finger touched my hand. "That which doesn't come or go: it is all that is, and all that is not. Present now and always. All is the same, always."

I quickly recognized that what was speaking and what was listening were the same; what was dying and what was living were the same. My eyes must have widened, as my sense of separateness dissolved into what is always present. He tapped my hand, smiled with a grimace, and laid back down.

I rose, and said aloud: "I need not fear!"

"Yes," he said with closed eyes.

Ananda glimpsed my feet, raised the curtain, waved me out, and went in. I parted, again, through the somber circle. Now tear's were appearing in my eyes too. Achitanaya walked with me, head bowed, to the pipal tree, where I took up the water pouch and rice ball. I bowed to him in thanks.

"Ananda said that Benai told him," Achit said falteringly, "the Tathagata will not see another sunrise. Between us, we will carry his body to Kusinara, where a pyre can be built. So, we will likely be there for two days. Then the master wants us to return to Vesali, where land was given for a winter encampment. I don't expect to return to Pava. Please tell my father that I will remain with the sangha." He continued:

"The master asked Benai, Ananda said, to tell my father about the accident, and to say 'accidents can happen to any one of us: we need feel neither remorse nor reproach. Accidents happen, and can happen to any of us. We need feel no sorrow.' So, assure my father that the Tathagata has died in peace, and he is grateful for the gifts bestowed on the monks. This is his message to my father: to find the lasting fulfillment that he seeks." Achit wiped his eyes. I responded:

"Yes, I will speak about the master, and how he died without fear or regret. I will then spend one day at the hermitage, and join you monks before you leave for Kusinara. I want to be with the sangha as it prepares the winter retreat. Will Ananda approve of my interest?," I queried.

"Yes. Yes." Achit seemed pleased.

We embraced as brothers, and I headed toward Pava, as the sun began to set for the master's last time – and for my first time, as his disciple.

* * *

Dear Reader,

Download free audio from the book, watch videos, share your thoughts and connect with others: visit www.livingnonduality.org/one-essence to explore.

Keep discovering,

Michael Lommel, publisher
Karina Library Press
michael@karinalibrary.com
P.O. Box 35
Ojai, California 93024

CPSIA information can be obtained at www.ICGtesting.com
Printed in the USA
LVOW011410170112

264281LV00004B/11/P